D1458047

better together*

*This book is best read together, grownup and kid.

akidsbookabout.com

a kids
book
about

™

a kids book about™

IMMIGRATION

by MJ Calderon

a
kids
book
about™

Text and design copyright © 2021
by A Kids Book About, Inc.

Copyright is good! It ensures that work like this can exist,
and more work in the future can be created.

All rights reserved. No part of this publication may be
reproduced, distributed, or transmitted in any form or
by any means, including photocopying, recording, other
electronic or mechanical methods, without the prior
written permission of the publisher, except in the case of
brief quotations embodied in critical reviews and certain
other noncommercial uses permitted by copyright law.
For permission requests, write to the publisher.

Printed in the United States of America.

A Kids Book About books are available online:
www.akidsbookabout.com

To share your stories, ask questions, or inquire about bulk
purchases (schools, libraries, and nonprofits), please use
the following email address:

hello@akidsbookabout.com

ISBN: 978-1-951253-79-0

Designed by Duke Stebbins
Edited by Denise Morales Soto

Dedicated to my mom, my real hero.

Intro

Understanding the world and those who inhabit it is a difficult and exhausting journey for everyone. Which is why grownups tend to make the mistake of tip-toeing around certain topics they have grown to better ignore rather than to take the time to ask questions and learn about it.

While immigration is an important topic, it's also a complicated one. Immigration often involves making hard decisions out of desperation, fear, and love, and it's often a very difficult journey that is driven by hope. So the goal of this book is not to become an expert on immigration, but to encourage discussion and to understand that we all contribute to making our country—and the world—a better place for everyone, ourselves included. No matter who we are, or where we come from, we all matter.

We are just human beings after all.

Immigration.

That's a big word, huh?

The meaning of it is even bigger.

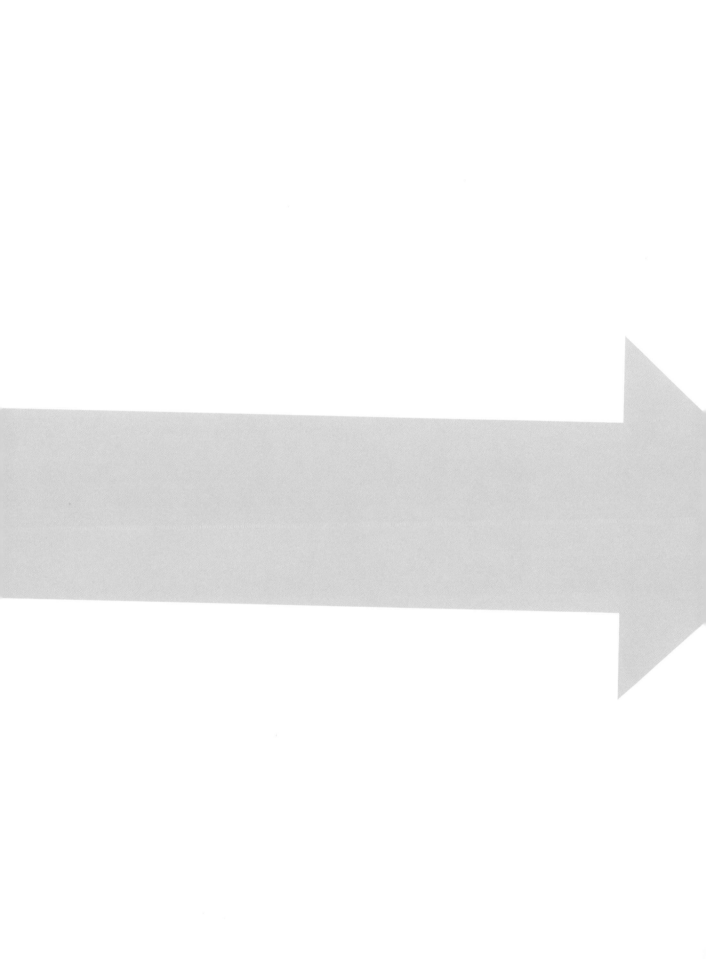

Immigration

is when you leave the country you were born in to live in another country.

Simple, right?
Well, not so fast.

There are lots of reasons why people choose to leave their home country...

Sometimes people move because they want to experience a different culture or live somewhere new— **but in most cases, the reasons are more complicated.**

Many people are pressured to make the difficult decision to leave their home country because they're running away from danger.

Sometimes they lack basic things like food, proper education, or medicine.

Sometimes, parents decide to leave their home country in order to give their children a better life.

A lot of times, people don't even want to leave their home, they just don't have any other options.

No matter the reason why you leave, when you move to another country, you are an **immigrant** —

like me and my family...

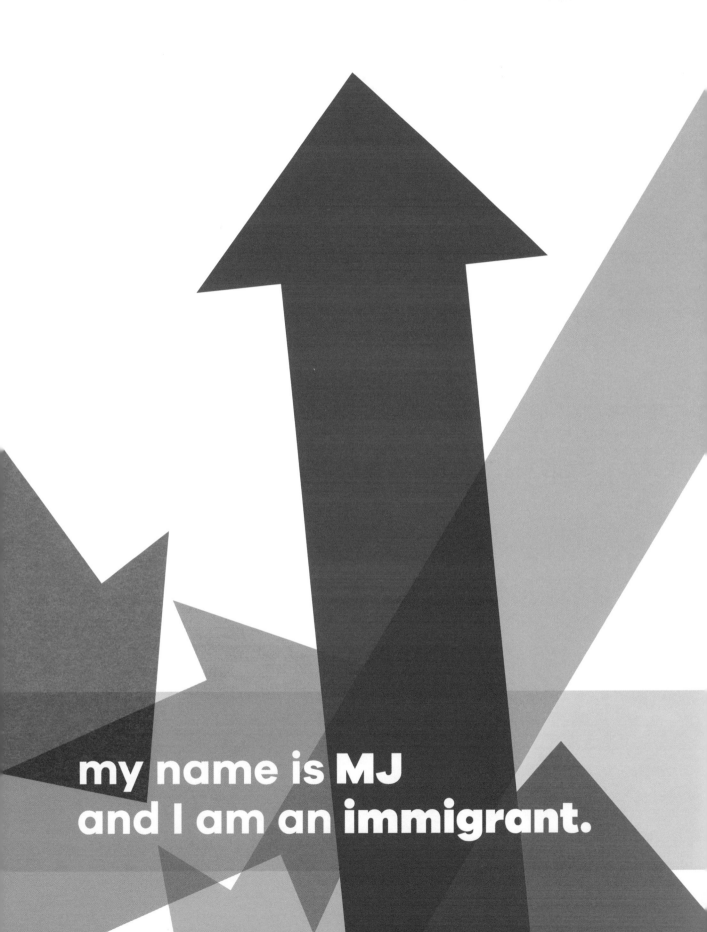

my name is **MJ**
and I am an **immigrant.**

My family and I are from Mexico.

When I was about 5 years old, my mother decided to come to the United States of America.

She was tired of struggling to live day-by-day in a dangerous city, with limited resources, and a lack of opportunities for her children.

Eventually, she made the difficult decision to leave me and my little brother behind to find that better life for us.

My mother worked 3 jobs
to save up enough money
to pay a "Coyote*" so
we could join her.

*a Coyote is a person that gets paid
to smuggle people from Mexico
into the United States of America.

Did you know, it's very hard to come into a country like the United States of America?

To come into the USA legally, there's a really long list of things you need to have, be, and do.

You need to have a lot of education, a bunch of money, maybe own land, and a lot of other stuff.

All these things are necessary just to be considered.

It's a really complicated process
and it takes a long long long long lo

ong long long long long long long long

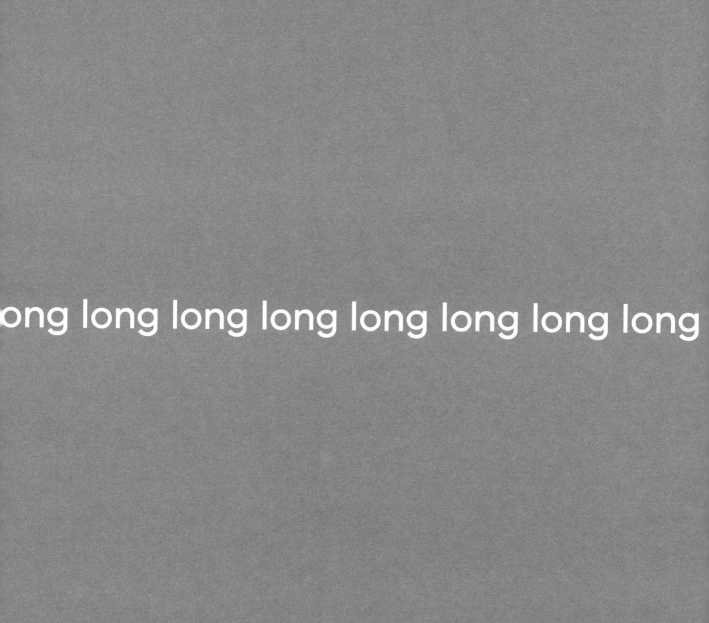

g long long long long long long time.

Sometimes it takes more than 10 years!

Most people looking to leave their country don't meet these requirements, and even if they do, they can still get denied.

There are no guarantees.

This often leaves people **desperate** and with no other option but to take a journey that is a lot harder and more dangerous.

Sometimes that journey
is physically dangerous
like it was for my mother
when she crossed the desert.

Other times that journey
is emotionally difficult like it
was for my brother and me.

While my mother had to deal with desert snakes and crossing a dangerous waterway,

we were badly bullied by many unkind strangers on our journey to our new home.

Often when we talk about immigrants and immigration, we hear words like

"illegal"
or
"alien."

Those words are
dehumanizing*
and are used to make
immigrants sound
like bad guys or
dangerous people.

*to dehumanize means to make
someone seem or feel less than human.

Calling immigrants those names makes immigration harder to talk about.

Which makes it difficult for immigrants to share their struggles, ask for help when they need it, and advocate for change.

So don't call us aliens, because immigrants don't come from another planet.*

And don't say illegal, because most of us aren't criminals.

*Unless you're Superman.
He's an immigrant AND an alien!

Some of us are just undocumented.*

*That means that they don't have all of the DOCUMENTS required to live in the new country.

Immigrants aren't bad!

Talking about immigration isn't bad either.

**So ask questions,
be curious,**
and if you know anyone
who is from a different
country don't be afraid
to ask about their...

language, culture, or story.

When you ask questions,
really listen!

Because there is so much
to **learn and discover**
when you do.

**But remember sometimes, people might
not want to talk about it, and that's OK too!**

Often young, undocumented immigrants feel out of place and are treated differently simply because of their legal status.*

*Legal status is a person's position in society according to the law. Someone's legal status determines what they can and cannot do in the place they live in.

That's the only thing
that people see you as.

But my legal status does not
define me or my worth.

Immigrants are all around us and come from all over the world.

There are immigrants who are doctors, nurses, teachers, artists, and anything else you can think of—there's nothing they can't do!

But most importantly

immigrants are brothers, sisters, moms, dads, and your friends.

My family is just like any other American family.

We argue about who gets to hold the TV remote.

We sit down and have dinner together.

We talk about sports.

And we disagree about our favorite celebrities.

Even though I wasn't born here, I care deeply about the community I live in.

I care about and contribute to this country because **this is my home too.**

The legal status of a person should not be used to stereotype or dehumanize anyone.

Oftentimes, mentioning it or bringing it up is unnecessary.

Everyone around you deserves to be treated with respect, fairness, and kindness.

At the end of the day, no matter where we came from or how we got here...

we're all just human beings.

I am not illegal.

I am not an alien.

I'm just

Outro

Now that you've finished reading this book, take some time to absorb and process everything that was discussed. Then, most importantly, talk about it! This book is here to help you start an open conversation about immigration and immigrants with both kids and grownups and begin the journey of learning more about them together.

Continue to educate yourselves and others on immigration, and remember that while it is important to ask questions, the value is in paying attention and really listening to the answers. Because knowledge allows for empathy and justice, and establishes a foundation of kindness and respect toward all human beings.

find
more
kids
books
about

community, diversity, adoption, autism, technology, money, climate change, suicide, sexual abuse, gender, and addiction.

akidsbookabout.com

share
your read*

*Tell somebody, post a photo, or give this book away to share what you care about.

@akidsbookabout